STEM ADVENTURES

EXTREME
ENGINEERING

First edition for the United States
and Canada published in 2018 by
Barron's Educational Series, Inc.

Text, design, and illustrations
copyright © Carlton Books Limited 2018,
an imprint of the Carlton Publishing Group,
20 Mortimer Street, London, W1T 3JW

All inquiries should be addressed to:
Barron's Educational Series, Inc.
250 Wireless Boulevard
Hauppauge, NY 11788
www.barronseduc.com

ISBN: 978-1-4380-1249-0

Date of Manufacture: July 2018
Manufactured by: RRD Asia, Dongguan, China

Printed in China
9 8 7 6 5 4 3 2 1

Executive editor: Bryony Davies
Design: Kate Wiliwinska
Designed and illustrated by: Dynamo Limited
Picture research: Steve Behan and Paul Langan
Production: Nicola Davey

AUTHOR:

PAUL VIRR has a long and diverse history of
working on children's books, including Carlton's Blue Peter
award-winning Countdown to the Olympic Games and
flagship children's guides for the top U.K. museums. He
has authored children's books on subjects ranging from
space and technology to dinosaurs. He is an official STEM
ambassador, having worked several years creating fun
STEM activity workshops for young scientists.

STEM EDITORIAL CONSULTANT:
MARGARET (MEG) KÄUFER is a

founding member and current president of the STEM
Alliance of Larchmont-Mamaroneck, NY. The STEM
Alliance is a nonprofit organization with the mission of
creating a network of STEM learning opportunities to
connect today's youth to the jobs of the future. They work
closely with local schools to run hands-on, applied STEM
enrichment experiences. Highlights of their work under
her leadership include launching an annual public STEM
festival, establishing competitive robotics teams, and
creating a hands-on STEM summer enrichment program
for at-risk children. Meg has her Masters in Curriculum &
Instruction from Teachers College, Columbia University.
Throughout her career, Meg has championed STEM
learning for its capacity to engage and inspire all
varieties of learners.

PICTURE ACKNOWLEDGMENTS

The publishers would like to thank the following sources for their kind
permission to reproduce the pictures in the book.

Pages 1, 3, 4–5 (backgrounds): Bioraven/Shutterstock; 6–7: Alexandr III/
Shutterstock; 8 (top right): Berti123/Shutterstock; 9 (top right): JingAiping/
Shutterstock, (bottom right): Taki O/Shutterstock; 10 (right): Atiger/
Shutterstock, (left, right & bottom center): Ctrl-x/Shutterstock, (bottom
left): Ksenvitaln/Shutterstock; 13 (top left): Andre Klopper/Shutterstock,
(top right): Lukiyanova Natalia frenta/Shutterstock; 16 (top right): Public
Domain; 17 (top left): R.M. Nunes/Shutterstock, (top right): John Loengard/
The LIFE Images Collection/Getty Images, (background): Yurachevsky/
Shutterstock; 20–21 (background): Bioraven/Shutterstock; 22 (bottom left):
Granger/REX/Shutterstock; 24 (top right): PI/Shutterstock; 30 (center):
Volodymyr Goinyk/Shutterstock; 33 (top): Onfilm/Getty Images; 34 (left):
Everett Historical/Shutterstock, (right): Pictorial Press Ltd/Alamy, (bottom
left): Granger Historical Picture Archive/Alamy, (bottom right): Science
History Images/Alamy; 36 (top left): Chones/Shutterstock, (center): Mifid/
Shutterstock; 38 (top right): Library of Congress; 40–41 (background):
Tovovan/Shutterstock; 40 (top right): Public Domain; 44 (top right): Public
Domain; 46 (top right): Cynthia Johnson/The LIFE Images Collection/Getty
Images; 48 (top right): Library of Congress, (left): Bettmann/Getty Images;
50 (top right): Chombosan/Shutterstock; 52–53 (background): Makc/
Shutterstock; 56 (top right): Science History Images/Alamy

Every effort has been made to acknowledge correctly and contact
the source and/or copyright holder of each picture, and Carlton Books
apologizes for any unintentional errors or omissions, which will be
corrected in future editions of this book.

STEM ADVENTURES

EXTREME
ENGINEERING

Paul Virr

BARRON'S

CONTENTS

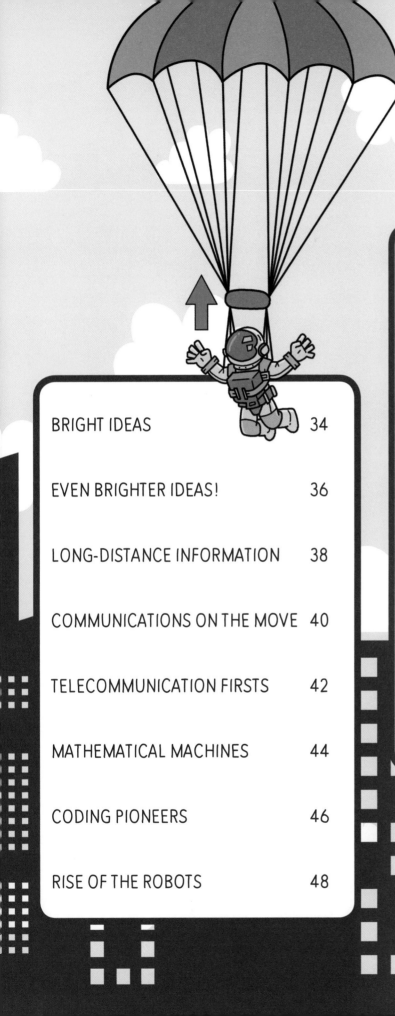

SUPER STEM

Welcome to the world of STEM. STEM stands for science, technology, engineering, and math. These four fabulous subjects open up a world of exciting discovery.

You probably already possess many of the qualities and interests shared by great scientists, technologists, engineers, and mathematicians. Read each statement and put a check in the box if it applies to you.

SCIENCE

You...

● are curious about the world around you. ☐

● love to ask questions. ☐

● experiment and try new things, even if it means making a mistake. ☐

You're already on your way to becoming a scientist! You're excited to discover more about the way scientists think and work.

TECHNOLOGY

You...

● are always playing with gadgets. ☐

● like to understand exactly how machines work. ☐

● try to find ways of making everyday tasks easier, such as investigating whether a different route to school makes the trip shorter. ☐

Technology is right up your alley! You're fascinated by the latest products and want to find out more about inventions that help improve our world.

ENGINEERING

You...

- like using your brain to solve problems. ☐

- love playing with construction sets and building blocks. ☐

- enjoy building amazing dens or dams in streams. ☐

You're perfectly suited to a career as an engineer! You could invent or make amazing tools, machines, and buildings.

MATH

You...

- like to understand the reasons why something is true. ☐

- often spot patterns in pictures and clothing or sequences in numbers like football statistics. ☐

- love 3-D puzzles, card games, and logic games like chess. ☐

You're a born mathematician! You're excited by shapes and measurements and curious to see what numbers can do when you use them in different ways.

WHAT IS ENGINEERING?

This book is all about engineering. Engineers are problem solvers who use science, math, and technology to make our world a better place. They use their skills and creativity to invent useful things, from everyday products, such as energy-saving light bulbs, to out-of-this world machines, such as space probes.

Engineers design processes or systems that solve problems or make things easier, such as building safe and efficient bicycle lanes in busy cities.

Once you start to look, you'll soon see that engineering is everywhere around you. The materials and the design of your skateboard and the phone in your pocket are all possible thanks to the work of countless engineers!

AWESOME ARCHES

Civil engineers build structures that shape and connect our world, such as buildings, roads, bridges, and railroads. They use strong shapes, such as arches, to help their structures stand up to gravity.

Arches can span a space without using lots of building material. Look at all the empty space in this structure!

The stone in the middle is called the keystone. It has sloped sides that allow it to slide into the middle of the arch, locking it together.

The Pont du Gard aqueduct in France carries water to towns in the area. It was built by Roman engineers nearly 2,000 years ago.

ACTIVITY

Complete the Roman arch by drawing lines from the spaces to the correct missing blocks.

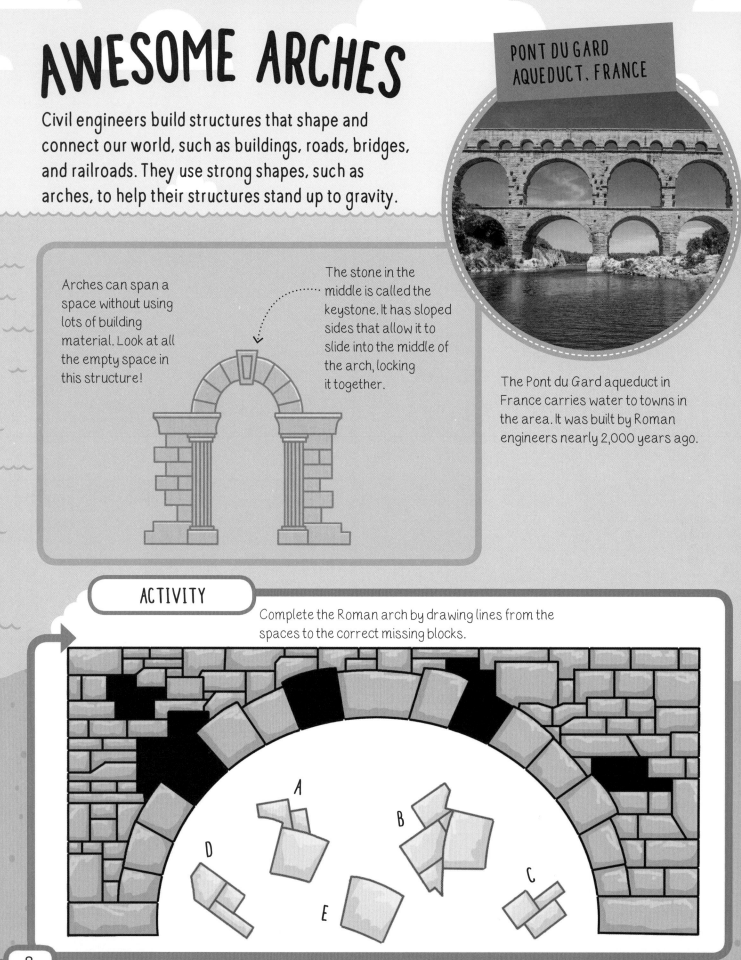

A

B

C

D

E

CHECK THE ANSWERS AT THE BACK OF THE BOOK!

Huge bridges are built all over the world, and they often become tourist attractions. Look at these half-drawn bridges—complete each bridge by sketching the other half, then color the pictures in.

CHAOTIANMEN BRIDGE, CHINA

This road and rail bridge is a whopping 1,811 feet (552 meters) long!

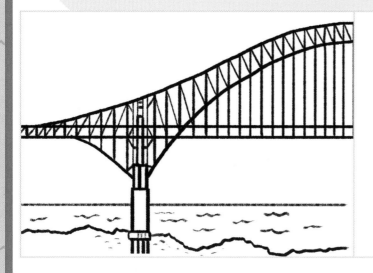

SYDNEY HARBOUR BRIDGE, AUSTRALIA

This bridge has been nicknamed "The Coat Hanger" because of its shape.

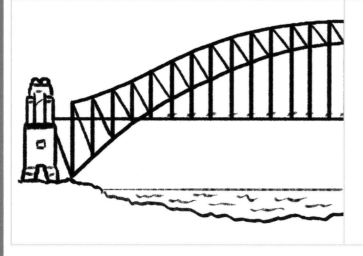

GREEN SKYSCRAPERS

The Shanghai Tower is an example of amazing engineering. It stands 2,073 feet (632 meters) high, and is a "green skyscraper," so it's friendly to the environment.

WHY IS THE TOWER SO GREEN?

There are 200 wind turbines at the top of the tower. They produce 10 percent of its electricity.

The tower has a twisted shape, which reduces the wind pressure on it. This means that less steel was needed to build it.

The tower has a double wall of glass around it, which helps maintain the temperature of the building.

There are 24 "sky gardens" built into the structure between the glass walls. All of those plants are good for the environment.

The tower collects rainwater and recycles waste water.

Design and draw your own green skyscraper. What features would you add to reduce waste or use renewable energy? What materials and shapes would you use? Will they be strong enough for your building to be tall?

MATERIALS USED:

- ✔ _____
- ✔ _____
- ✔ _____
- ✔ _____
- ✔ _____
- ✔ _____
- ✔ _____
- ✔ _____
- ✔ _____
- ✔ _____
- ✔ _____
- ✔ _____
- ✔ _____
- ✔ _____
- ✔ _____

The Bosco Verticale in Milan, Italy, has two towers. They contain 100 apartments and a "vertical forest" planted with 20,000 trees and smaller plants. All of this greenery turns 44,000 pounds of carbon dioxide into oxygen every year, and it filters out dust and pollution.

SEESAW SCIENCE

Engineers build machines that make doing work easier. You might think a machine is always something complex, like a car. But some machines, such as levers, are very simple.

A lever makes it easier to lift things. It is a rigid bar balanced on a raised edge called a pivot or a fulcrum.

A seesaw is a type of lever. The fulcrum is in the middle of the bar.

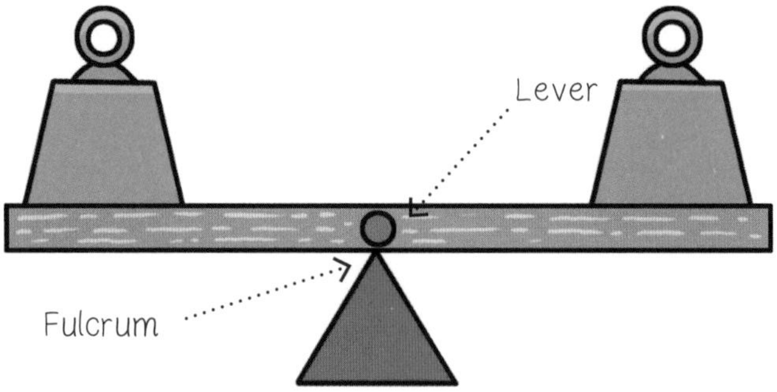

Lever

Fulcrum

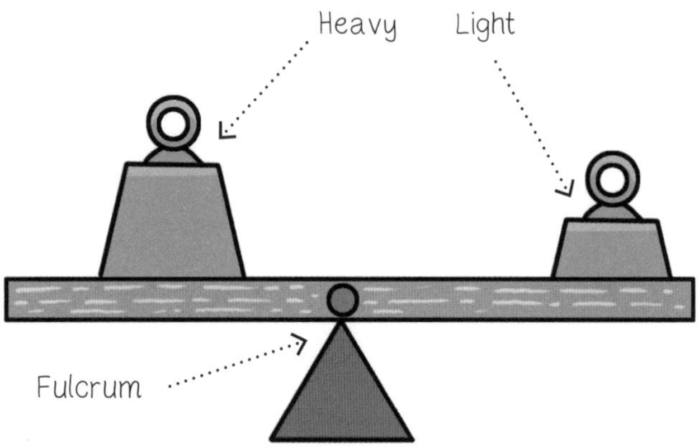

Heavy   Light

Fulcrum

A heavy object close to the fulcrum can balance a lighter object that is farther away.

Draw arrows above the elephants on each of the seesaws below to show which side will go up and which will go down! If the seesaw balances, draw an equal sign (=).

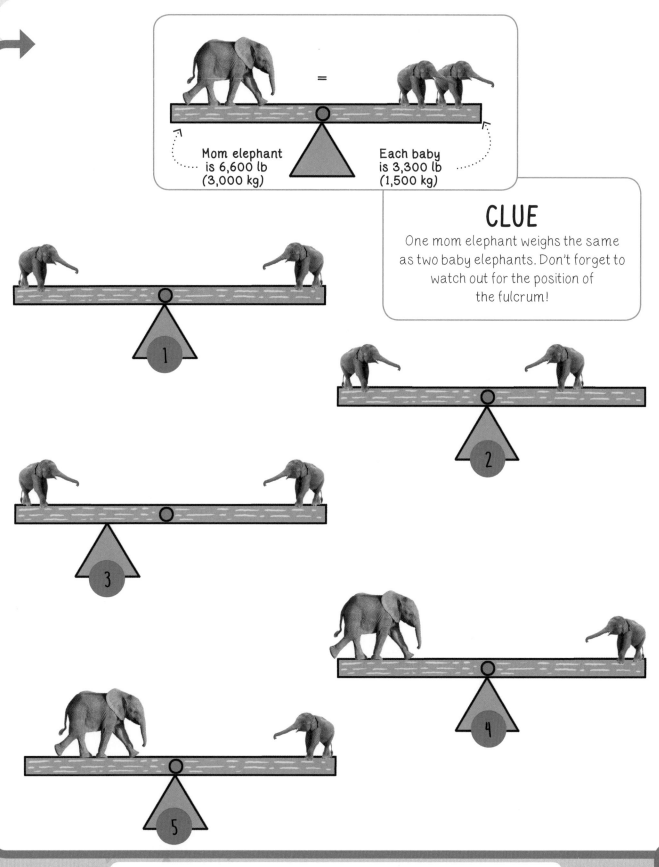

Mom elephant is 6,600 lb (3,000 kg)

Each baby is 3,300 lb (1,500 kg)

CLUE

One mom elephant weighs the same as two baby elephants. Don't forget to watch out for the position of the fulcrum!

LEVERS TO LIFT

Seesaws aren't the only kind of lever—wheelbarrows are too! They make things much easier to lift.

> The load is between the effort and the fulcrum.

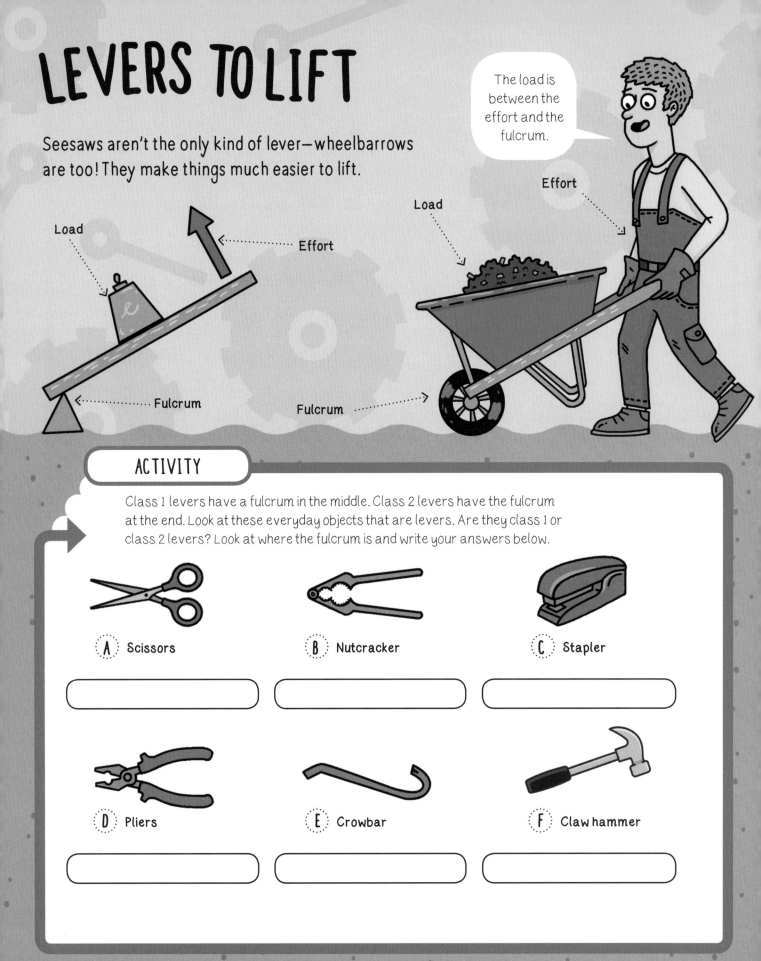

Load

Effort

Fulcrum

Load

Effort

Fulcrum

ACTIVITY

Class 1 levers have a fulcrum in the middle. Class 2 levers have the fulcrum at the end. Look at these everyday objects that are levers. Are they class 1 or class 2 levers? Look at where the fulcrum is and write your answers below.

A) Scissors

B) Nutcracker

C) Stapler

D) Pliers

E) Crowbar

F) Claw hammer

CHECK THE ANSWERS AT THE BACK OF THE BOOK!

YOUR BODY IS A SPORTS MACHINE

Your arm can also be a lever. In this type of lever, your arm doesn't make things easier to lift. Instead, your arm multiplies speed.

When you throw a ball, your arm acts like a lever to throw the baseball a greater distance—basically making it FASTER.

DID YOU KNOW?

Materials engineers create sports equipment to help athletes get better and better.

ACTIVITY

Give these sports players' mechanical advantage! Pick the correct piece of equipment from the blue panel on the right. Each one is a lever! Draw the correct gear for each player.

RAISE THE ROOF

Structural engineers carefully choose the shapes they build with. Domes are cool shapes. They defy gravity, so it looks like there's nothing holding them up!

The Pantheon is a building in Rome that was built by engineers nearly 2,000 years ago. It has a huge dome, and it's still standing! How did they manage this?

1. They used heavy materials at the bottom of the dome and lighter materials at the top.

2. They made the walls thicker at the bottom and thinner at the top.

3. They left a large circular opening—an "oculus"— at the top to reduce weight.

4. They "coffered" the ceiling—a technique of using thin, light squares in the dome.

THE PANTHEON

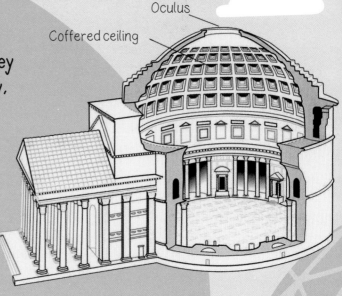

Oculus

Coffered ceiling

ACTIVITY

Can you find a route across the coffered dome of the Pantheon? You can only travel through the solid colored blocks.

FINISH

START

GEODESIC DOMES

Engineering ideas get better and better as people build on earlier ideas. In the 1940s, a new form of dome was created.

It was invented by R. Buckminster Fuller and called the geodesic dome. It is built from super-strong triangles. These are stronger shapes than rectangles.

R. BUCKMINSTER FULLER
was an early environmentalist and green pioneer who also invented energy efficient vehicles.

ACTIVITY

Can you construct your own geodesic dome by completing the missing triangles?

A SCREWY IDEA?

It's very dry in Egypt and doesn't rain much there, so farmers need to bring water to their crops through irrigation (using water channels). The channels are close by but lower than the fields. Water doesn't flow uphill, so that requires an engineering solution called the Archimedes screw!

ACTIVITY

Will the water reach all of the farmer's olive trees? Starting in the bottom corner, color in the channels leading from the black arrow to show how many trees will be irrigated.

The Archimedes screw can move water from a low point to a higher point. Turning the screw with the handle draws water up the hollow pipe.

The water is lifted uphill with minimal effort. It pours out of the top into the fields.

WATER POWER!

Some civil engineers design and build power stations. Hydroelectric power stations use the high energy of water rushing downhill to produce electricity. The water turns a propeller-like wheel called a turbine as it rushes past. A generator converts this rotating motion into electricity.

Hydroelectric power stations produce what is known as clean electricity. This is because they don't need to burn environmentally damaging fossil fuels, such as coal.

ACTIVITY

The top picture shows all of the parts of a hydropower plant. But there are 5 differences in the bottom picture. Can you spot them and circle them?

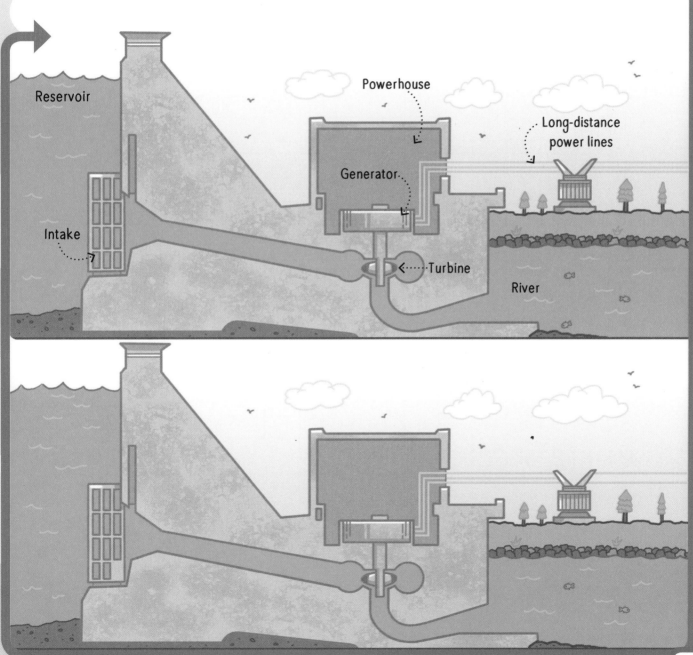

Reservoir

Powerhouse

Long-distance power lines

Generator

Intake

Turbine

River

TALL IS COOL

Civil engineers know their materials, especially when they build skyscrapers! Some materials need to be strong and rigid, like the steel frame of a tall building, while others need to be light and flexible, such as plastic pipes to carry water.

ACTIVITY

See how many building materials you can find in this skyscraper word search.

A	K	J	C	E	M	E	N	T	G	P	L	A	S	T	E	R
T	G	C	O	N	C	R	E	T	E	L	C	M	A	X	S	W
R	E	W	Z	X	C	V	U	J	N	G	O	F	I	M	J	O
T	E	D	S	W	Q	A	X	U	I	N	P	J	K	M	T	O
A	L	U	M	I	N	U	M	I	A	X	P	B	V	M	J	D
G	T	Y	U	I	O	L	K	J	E	R	E	D	S	Q	W	P
Z	X	B	N	M	T	F	G	D	F	I	R	J	K	H	Y	L
G	L	A	S	S	R	T	Y	U	G	F	D	D	B	N	V	A
K	L	O	T	Z	X	C	R	E	W	D	S	T	E	E	L	S
R	E	W	O	A	S	M	N	H	N	M	J	G	F	U	V	T
A	O	P	N	K	U	J	M	V	B	C	X	Z	T	R	L	I
G	L	U	E	W	P	K	L	I	U	X	Y	H	Q	T	G	C
O	I	B	R	I	C	K	E	D	W	F	S	A	N	D	K	M

CONCRETE   GLASS   CEMENT
STEEL   WOOD   PLASTER
ALUMINUM   STONE   GLUE
COPPER   BRICK
PLASTIC   SAND

WHAT ARE CIVIL ENGINEERS?

Civil engineers design systems for everything around us—from schools and hospitals to roads, railroads, and bridges, and our water and power supplies. They build, and keep running, things that we depend on every day.

CHECK THE ANSWERS AT THE BACK OF THE BOOK!

If you want to build a tall building, you're going to need a tower crane! Tower cranes lift heavy materials, tools, and even prebuilt sections of buildings. They use levers and pulleys to get the job done.

ACTIVITY

Can you put the labels in the correct place on the crane? We've started for you. Read the labels carefully to help you.

7

3

1. Cab: this is up high, where the crane's operator sits!

2. Horizontal jib: the arm of the crane, which swings around

3. Counterweight: balances the weight of the load on the opposite side of the jib

4. Load: what the crane carries

5. Base weights: weights that steady the crane

6. Tower: gives the crane its height

7. Trolley: moves the load along the jib

TAKE THE ELEVATOR

Skyscrapers created compact living and office space on a small footprint by building upward. But it's not much fun living on the top floor if you have to take the stairs! Luckily, engineers invented a quicker vertical mode of transport—the elevator. Look at where elevators are headed next: SPACE!

1

The first elevator was built by ancient Greek inventor Archimedes more than 2,000 years ago. Early elevators probably used ropes and pulleys.

2

In 1852, an engineer named Elisha Otis designed a safety elevator. If the cable snapped, the cab would automatically stop, instead of fall. Steam-powered and motorized elevators needed these safety mechanisms.

3

The first vacuum elevator, which uses air pressure to move a cab up and down, went on sale in Argentina in 2000.

4

Today, scientists are working to build a space elevator that is anchored on Earth and connected to an endpoint in space that orbits with Earth.

The idea was first proposed in 1895 by Russian rocket scientist Tsiolkovsky, but it might come true in the future!

ACTIVITY

Ellie rides the elevator from the ground floor to the floor where she lives, without pressing any buttons. Read the details of her journey, and see if you can figure out what floor she lives on.

Ellie gets in the elevator and meets Anne, who is already on board. Ellie rides up five floors, and Anne gets off.

Bill gets in, goes down two floors, and gets out.

Cara gets in, goes up nine floors, and gets out.

The elevator goes down two floors, and a group of schoolchildren get in.

The elevator goes down another three floors, and the children get off.

An old lady with a dog gets in, goes up one floor, and she gets out with her dog.

Bea gets in, goes down six floors, and gets out.

Ellie gets out, too!

What floor does Ellie live on?

GOING UNDERGROUND

When a giant obstacle gets in the way of your transport project, what do you do? One answer is to tunnel underneath it! Going underground is a great engineering solution if you want to build a new train line across a busy city, some massive mountains, or a large body of water!

A "BORING" TUNNEL FACT

The Gotthard Base Tunnel was built using a combination of tunnel boring machines (TBMs) and dynamite. Boom! Four TBMs were used at the same time, and each one dug out up to 98 feet (30 meters) a day.

The Gotthard Base Tunnel in Switzerland opened in 2016. It has two one-way tubes that run underneath the Alp mountains. It is the world's longest and deepest train tunnel, with a length of 35 miles (57 kilometers). Over 200 trains travel through the tunnel every day at speeds of 155 mph (250 kmh).

Over 28,200,000 tons of rock were excavated. That's about the same as five Great Pyramids!

Two tunnels are linked every 980 feet (300 meters) so that passengers can escape to the other tunnel in case of an emergency.

The tunnels have sensors to detect if there are any structural problems.

ACTIVITY

Go underground to discover the lengths
of these famous train tunnels.

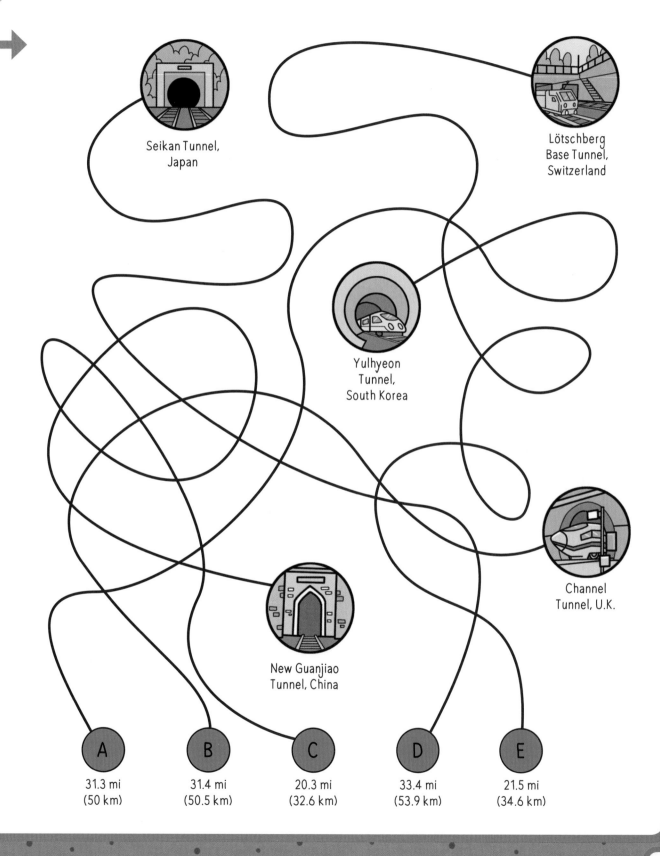

Seikan Tunnel,
Japan

Lötschberg
Base Tunnel,
Switzerland

Yulhyeon
Tunnel,
South Korea

Channel
Tunnel, U.K.

New Guanjiao
Tunnel, China

A
31.3 mi
(50 km)

B
31.4 mi
(50.5 km)

C
20.3 mi
(32.6 km)

D
33.4 mi
(53.9 km)

E
21.5 mi
(34.6 km)

CHECK THE ANSWERS AT THE BACK OF THE BOOK!

WORLD OF WHEELS

Imagine what a drag the world would be without wheels—literally! You'd have to drag stuff around against the force of friction. But thankfully, we have wheels to help us. A wheel on an axle is a simple machine that reduces friction.

1 The first wheels were solid wooden disks with holes for the wooden axles to pass through. They helped chariots and wagons roll along, but the ride must have been bumpy!

Wooden wheels with spokes were developed around 2,000 B.C., and continued to be used into the 19th century.

2 Wire-spoked wheels were lightweight, stiff, and strong. They were used for the huge wheels at the front of Penny Farthing bicycles.

3 The first practical motor car had wheels with solid rubber tires. These absorbed some of the impact of rough roads.

4 Trains with steel-spoked wheels that ran on steel tracks could go really, really fast, thanks to reduced friction. In 1938, The Mallard made a record-breaking speed of 126 mph (203 kmh) to become the world's fastest steam train.

5 Designed to drive on the dusty and rocky surface of the moon, the Lunar Roving Vehicle had lightweight aluminum wheels with tires made of woven steel wires. These were covered with titanium chevrons to give them extra grip.

6 In the late 19th century, pneumatic tires were developed—rubber tires filled with compressed air (like you probably have on your car). These have good contact with the ground for traction, but they are flexible and provide extra suspension—for a less bumpy ride!

Wheels come in all shapes and sizes. Every wheel in this picture has an identical partner—except one. Can you spot it?

Future tires may not be pneumatic at all. One idea that has been developed uses flexible spokes that can bend and absorb impacts, just like a tire filled with air—but you can't get a flat tire!

AMAZING PARACHUTES

On October 24, 2014, Alan Eustace set a new world record for the highest parachute jump. He jumped 135,890 feet (41,419 meters) from a balloon at the edge of space! He made a safe landing, largely thanks to the technology of the parachute.

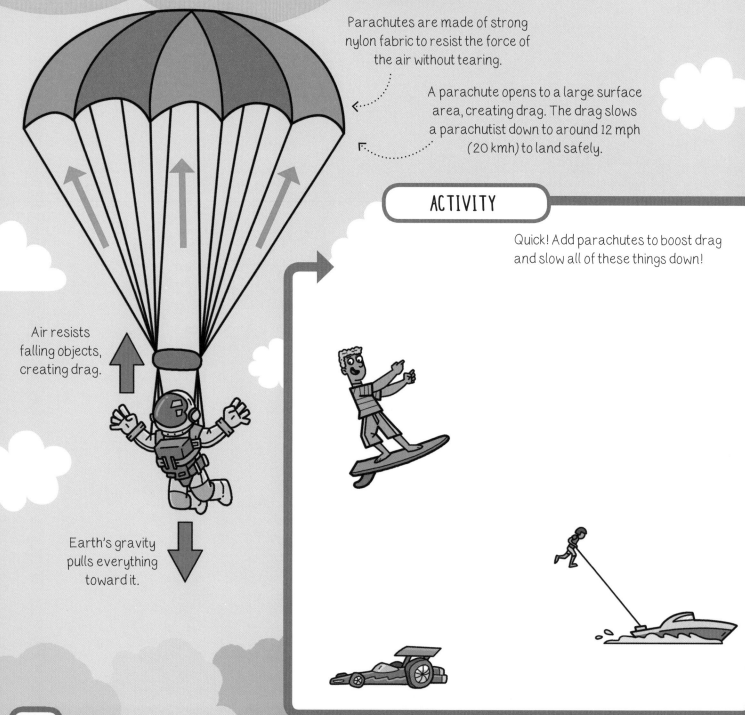

Parachutes are made of strong nylon fabric to resist the force of the air without tearing.

A parachute opens to a large surface area, creating drag. The drag slows a parachutist down to around 12 mph (20 kmh) to land safely.

Air resists falling objects, creating drag.

Earth's gravity pulls everything toward it.

ACTIVITY

Quick! Add parachutes to boost drag and slow all of these things down!

FLYING FIRSTS

Engineers often build on the work of earlier engineers to make new inventions and discoveries. Complex machines, such as modern airplanes, are possible due to the work of many aeronautic engineering pioneers!

ACTIVITY

Can you match the entries in this list of aeronautic engineering firsts with the icons that best represent them? Draw a line between each picture and the correct text.

A

1 The Montgolfier brothers' hot-air balloon made its first flight with passengers in 1783.

B

2 Louis-Sébastien Lenormand invented (and tested) the first working parachute in 1793.

C

D

3 George Cayley's heavier-than-air glider made a ground-breaking flight in 1853. He crash-landed!

E

4 The first rigid airship took to the skies in 1900. It was a large gas-filled balloon with a metal structure.

F

G

BOOM!

H

5 The first controlled flight in a powered, fixed-wing airplane was made by the Wright brothers in their Flyer airplane in 1903.

6 In 1932, Amelia Earhart became the first female aviator to make a solo flight across the Atlantic Ocean, flying from America to Ireland in a single-engine plane.

7 The first practical helicopter, Igor Sikorsky's VS 300, took off in 1940.

8 Chuck Yeager flew faster than the speed of sound, creating a sonic boom in a Bell X-1 jet in 1947.

CHECK THE ANSWERS AT THE BACK OF THE BOOK!

BUOYANT BALLOONS

The Montgolfier brothers' hot-air balloon was the first flying vehicle to carry people. Hot-air balloons still carry people into the skies today, but how do they get off the ground?

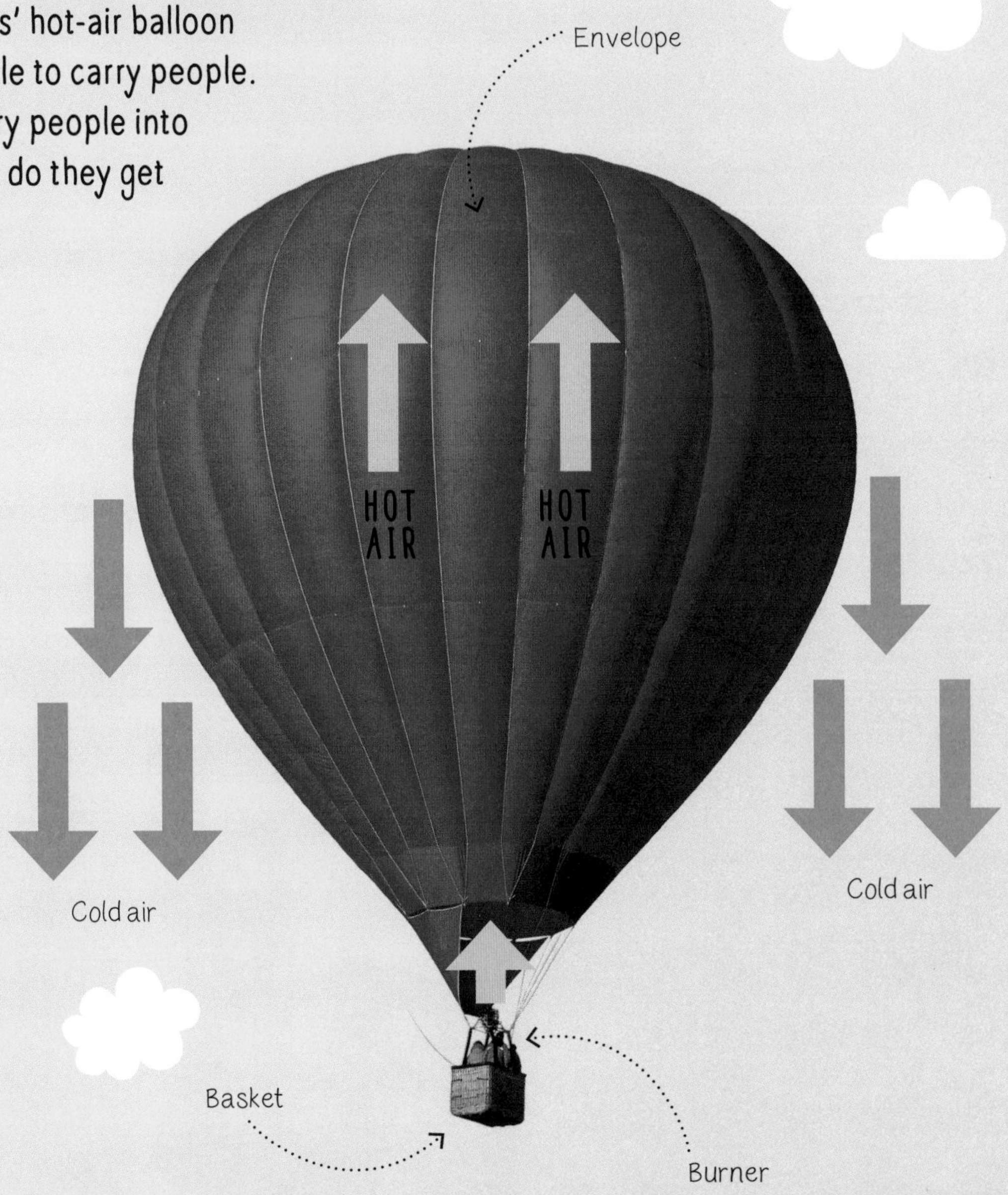

Envelope

HOT AIR

HOT AIR

Cold air

Cold air

Buoyancy does not just explain how things float on water. Hot-air balloons use it to float on air. The hot air trapped inside the balloon rises because the pressure of denser cold air surrounding it forces it upward.

Basket

Burner

It takes almost 216,000 square feet (20,000 square meters) of hot air to lift 1,000 pounds (450 kilograms), which is why hot-air balloons need to be huge!

Today, aeronautic engineers use strong, air-tight nylon for modern hot-air balloon envelopes.

Which way is each of these balloons headed—and why? Read the caption, and then draw an arrow by each balloon to show whether the balloon will travel up or down, or in another direction.

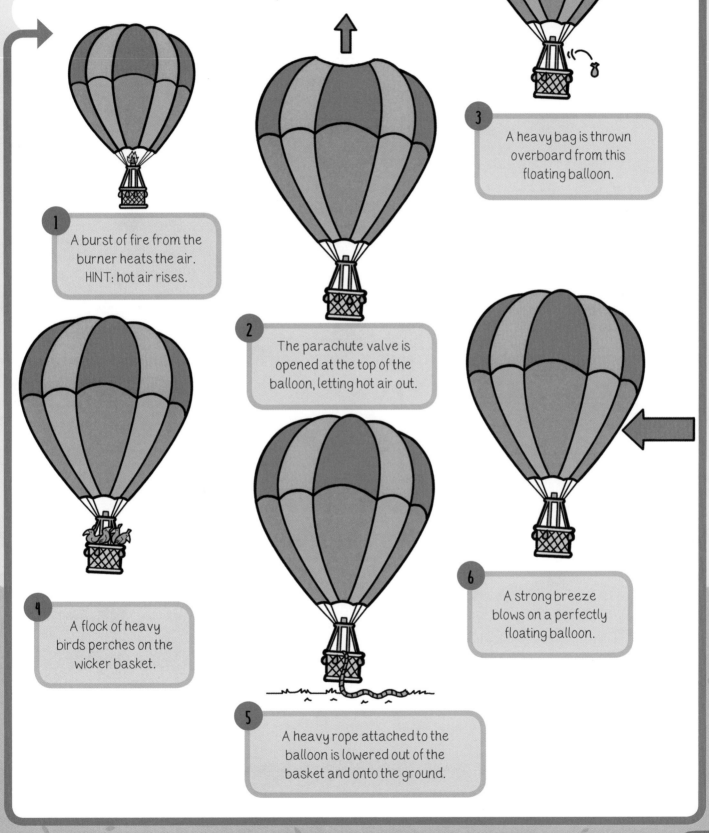

1 A burst of fire from the burner heats the air. HINT: hot air rises.

2 The parachute valve is opened at the top of the balloon, letting hot air out.

3 A heavy bag is thrown overboard from this floating balloon.

4 A flock of heavy birds perches on the wicker basket.

5 A heavy rope attached to the balloon is lowered out of the basket and onto the ground.

6 A strong breeze blows on a perfectly floating balloon.

SKATEPARK SCIENCE

A skateboard is a highly engineered machine, combining a mix of materials and technology that harness the energy of the skater and the forces of motion for the ride—and for tricks.

ACTIVITY

Gravity, friction, and forces of motion all play a part in the classic skateboard trick called the ollie. Read the captions below to discover the science behind the moves, and then number the images to put the steps in order (we've given you the first and last steps to get you started).

①

○

○

⑦ ___

○ ___

○ ___

○ ___

1 The skater rolls forward in a crouched position. The weight of the rider and the board is balanced by the ground pushing up.

2 The skater's right leg pushes the back of the board down. The rear axle acts as a pivot, and the front of the board starts to lift slightly.

3 The front of the board lifts even more, and the back of the board hits the ground. In reaction, the ground bounces it up into the air.

4 The board is in the air! The skater slides a foot forward, and friction pulls the board up with the skater.

5 In midair, the skater pushes down with his front foot, starting to make the board level.

6 The skater has both feet on the board as it reaches its maximum height, and gravity takes over.

7 The board and skater return to the ground, and momentum continues to carry them forward.

CHECK THE ANSWERS AT THE BACK OF THE BOOK!

Ramps are used by skaters wanting to catch some air or pick up some speed, but did you know that a ramp is considered a simple machine by engineers? Ramps certainly give skaters a mechanical advantage!

Ramps have been used since ancient times. About 4,500 years ago, before cranes were invented, Egyptians used extensive ramp systems to move heavy materials to build the pyramids.

ACTIVITY

Imagine you're whizzing along on your skateboard. What would happen if you encounter each of the following on your ride? Check the correct answer.

1. **You approach a very steep ramp at an angle of 70 degrees. It's stunt jump time. Cool!**

   ○ You slow down quickly, then stop.

   ○ Crash landing!

2. **You come to a set of steps going upward.**

   ○ Get ready to catch some air!

   ○ You're going to slow down, nice and gently.

   ○ Steps go up, but not so smoothly. Ouch! That hurts.

3. **There's a ramp with a 45-degree angle in front of you.**

   ○ Get ready to catch some air!

   ○ It's going to be a bumpy ride.

   ○ You're slowing down too quickly for a jump.

33

BRIGHT IDEAS

The light bulb is a great example to show how many great engineering minds improve a product over time. Nowadays, we barely notice what an amazing thing the light bulb is, but it's the sum of the work of lots of engineers.

INCANDESCENT LIGHT BULBS

Incandescent light bulbs work when electrical current passes through a piece of thin metal inside it, called a filament. The filament glows—turning electrical energy into light and heat.

Filament

1 THOMAS EDISON (1847–1931)

Edison tested a light bulb in 1879, which had a filament made of carbon. This is often thought of as the first practical light bulb. But the filaments broke, so the bulbs were not long lasting.

2 JOSEPH SWAN (1828–1914)

Swan was working on his own version of a light bulb at the same time as Edison, but Swan had created one slightly earlier. His bulbs had a very short life span, but his house was the first in the world with electric lights.

3 LEWIS HOWARD LATIMER (1848–1928)

Latimer came up with a new way to make the carbon filaments in a light bulb, which made them last longer. He also installed public electric lights in cities, including New York and London.

4 WILLIAM D. COOLIDGE (1873–1975)

Coolidge discovered a way to make a metal called tungsten more malleable—which meant he could bend it to be used inside light bulb filaments. It makes light bulbs brighter. These light bulbs went on sale in 1911.

Parts of each light bulb are missing. Can you match the missing part in the panel below to each light bulb? Draw a line between each bulb and the correct missing part.

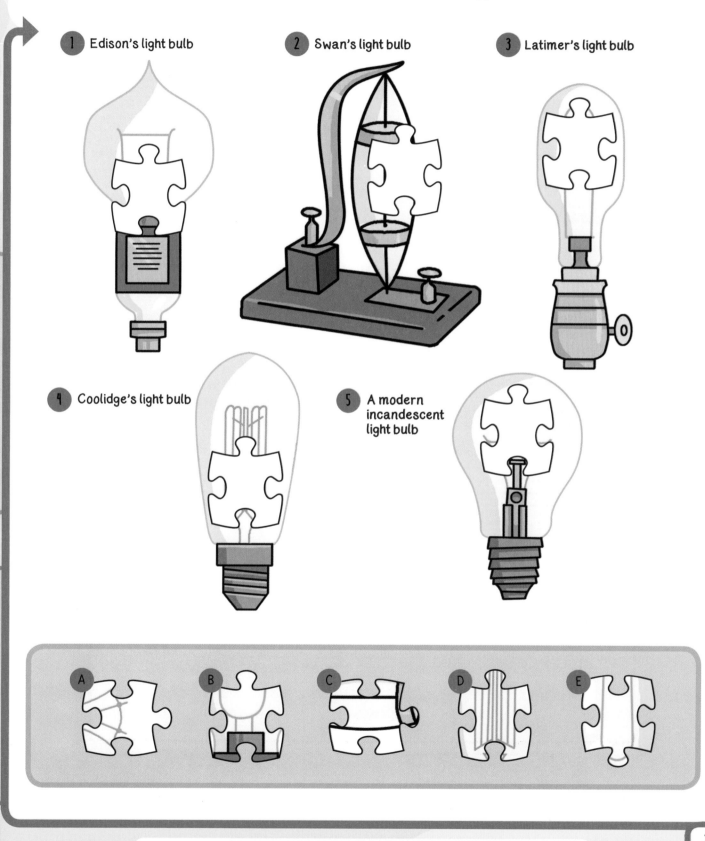

1 Edison's light bulb

2 Swan's light bulb

3 Latimer's light bulb

4 Coolidge's light bulb

5 A modern incandescent light bulb

A   B   C   D   E

EVEN BRIGHTER IDEAS!

A different way of converting electricity into light was developed more recently. In 1962, Nick Holonyak Jr. made the first light-emitting diode (LED) that could turn electrical inputs into visible red light.

Lens to direct the light

LED chip

Anode (positive) lead to battery

Cathode (negative) lead to battery

LED light bulbs convert electricity into light very efficiently. They cut energy use by more than 80 percent.

LEDs can provide 25,000 hours of light in their life span—that's more than three years of continuous use!

After red LEDs, yellow, blue, and white LEDs were soon created, which made LED light bulbs possible.

LEDs have no fragile filament to break and don't create much heat, so they last 25 times longer than old-fashioned light bulbs.

ACTIVITY

LED lights are often used in billboards for advertisements because they create bright screens. Can you design your own billboard advertising LED light bulbs?

ACTIVITY

Each dot in this billboard is an LED light bulb. Color the squares in to match the dots. What is revealed when it is switched on?

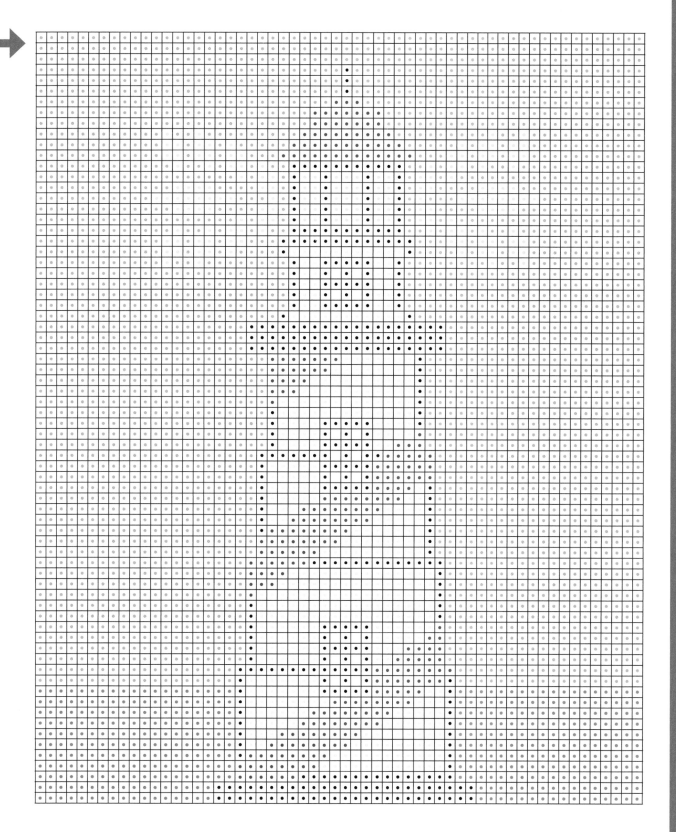

LONG-DISTANCE INFORMATION

Long before the smartphone, people communicated over long distances with text messages, but back then they were called codes. Lots of engineers thought about ways to do this, but it was Samuel Morse, and his assistant Alfred Vail, who set up a working telegraph system in 1837.

SAMUEL MORSE

Morse wasn't only an inventor. He was also a professional artist.

An electric telegraph uses electrical signals to send messages down a metal wire.

Morse and Vail developed a code of short and long signals, known as dots and dashes. The sender used a special key to tap in the dots and dashes. At the other end of the wire, a mechanism punched the dots and dashes onto paper, ready to be decoded!

ACTIVITY

On May 24, 1844, the first official Morse telegraph opened. Morse sent the first message a distance of around 40 miles (65 kilometers) from Washington, D.C. to Baltimore. Which wire should he use to get his message to Baltimore?

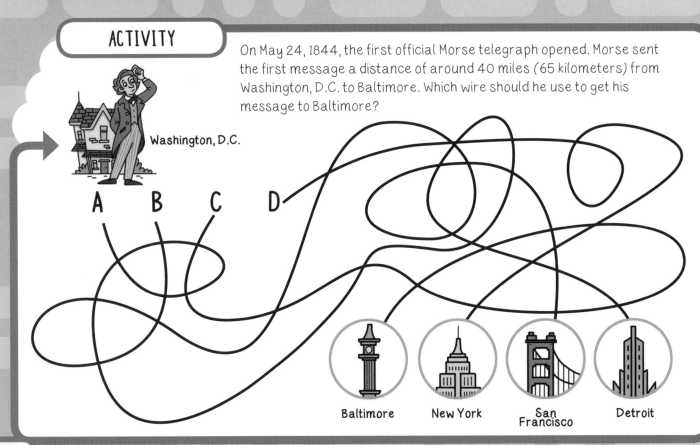

Washington, D.C.

A   B   C   D

Baltimore   New York   San Francisco   Detroit

CHECK THE ANSWERS AT THE BACK OF THE BOOK!

Use the Morse code key to decode and read
the first message that was sent by Morse.

MORE MORSE MESSAGES

Morse code signals can also be made
using sounds or flashes of light. Why not
send your own Morse code messages to
a friend using a flashlight?

CHECK THE ANSWERS AT THE BACK OF THE BOOK!

COMMUNICATIONS ON THE MOVE

The electric telegraph was an amazing invention. But what happened when someone wanted to send a message to something that was moving, like a train? In 1887, Granville Tailer Woods came up with a solution!

GRANVILLE T. WOODS

Woods was a mechanical and civil engineer. He was self-taught, with no official training, and he loved to invent things.

ACTIVITY

Can you connect the dots to finish the picture?

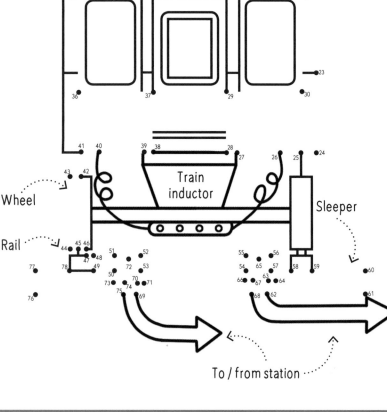

GUARD'S VAN

Wheel

Rail

Train inductor

Sleeper

To / from station

TELEGRAPHS AND TRAINS

In the late 19th century, train accidents were a big problem. Woods invented a way for trains and stations to send telegraph messages to each other. It let stations know where trains were and warned of problems on the line ahead.

The Synchronous Multiplex Railway Telegraph let an electrical signal pass between a train and lines laid between the tracks.

There's going to be a crash! Send some telegraph messages to stop it. First, trace a telegraph message through the maze from Train A to the station, to tell the stationmaster where it is.

Then quickly send another message from the station to Train B to tell it to stop.

TRAIN A

STATION

TRAIN B

CHECK THE ANSWERS AT THE BACK OF THE BOOK!

TELECOMMUNICATION FIRSTS

Engineers help keep us all in touch with the world, from chatting with friends to making lifesaving emergency calls. From the electric telegraph to a smartphone that can access the Internet, this field of engineering changed how people communicate with each other.

ACTIVITY

Each numbered fact on this page has a partner fact on page 43. Can you match them up? Read the text and look at the pictures for clues!

1858
Messages were first sent across the Atlantic using copper cable. The first message was in Morse code and took 17 hours to transmit, but this was a huge improvement on the 10 days it took a ship to carry a message!

1

1876
Alexander Graham Bell made the world's first telephone call to his assistant, Thomas Watson, who was waiting in the next room!

2

1901
Italian engineer Guglielmo Marconi built a wireless telegraphy system that he used to send signals across the Atlantic—without a cable. This was a major breakthrough for communications between ships at sea.

3

2007
The first smartphone with a touchscreen, rather than a keypad, went on sale. Smartphones have more processing power than the computers that helped NASA land astronauts on the moon!

6

1973
The first call was made from a handheld cell phone. It was large and heavy, weighing more than 2 pounds (1 kilogram). Early mobile phones became available to buy in 1984, but they were very expensive.

4

1992
Software engineer Neil Papworth sent the world's first text message from his computer to a cell phone. His message was a simple Christmas greeting.

5

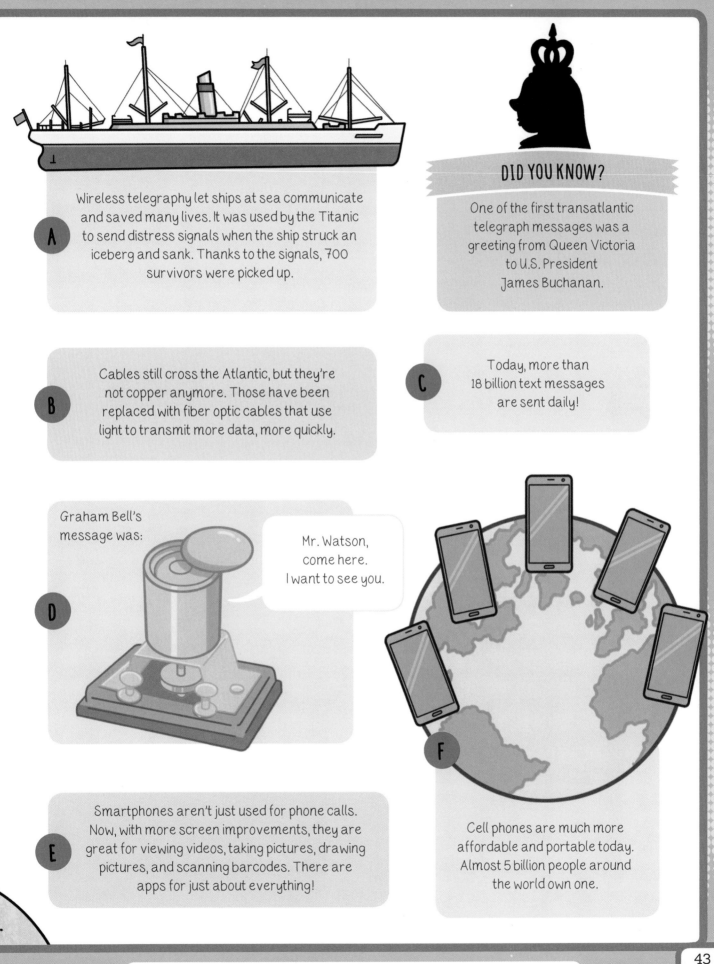

A Wireless telegraphy let ships at sea communicate and saved many lives. It was used by the Titanic to send distress signals when the ship struck an iceberg and sank. Thanks to the signals, 700 survivors were picked up.

DID YOU KNOW?

One of the first transatlantic telegraph messages was a greeting from Queen Victoria to U.S. President James Buchanan.

B Cables still cross the Atlantic, but they're not copper anymore. Those have been replaced with fiber optic cables that use light to transmit more data, more quickly.

C Today, more than 18 billion text messages are sent daily!

Graham Bell's message was:

Mr. Watson, come here. I want to see you.

D

E Smartphones aren't just used for phone calls. Now, with more screen improvements, they are great for viewing videos, taking pictures, drawing pictures, and scanning barcodes. There are apps for just about everything!

F Cell phones are much more affordable and portable today. Almost 5 billion people around the world own one.

CHECK THE ANSWERS AT THE BACK OF THE BOOK!

MATHEMATICAL MACHINES

Most projects need teams of people working together to come up with a great new engineering solution. When a mathematician named Ada Lovelace met mechanical engineer Charles Babbage in 1833, it was the start of a collaboration that led to the birth of computer science and software engineering.

ADA LOVELACE
Lovelace was taught math and science from the age of four. This was very unusual for a girl in the 1800s.

Babbage built a machine, called the Analytical Engine, to perform math calculations. It used rods, wheels, and cogs to add, subtract, multiply, and divide.

She designed a program on a series of cards with holes in them to input these instructions. Early electric computers would use the same method of inputting instructions and data!

Lovelace realized what it could do, and came up with a way to give it instructions—she wrote the world's first computer program.

The punched cards were modeled after the cards that were used to weave complex patterns on mechanical looms.

ACTIVITY

Can you spot 5 differences between these machines?

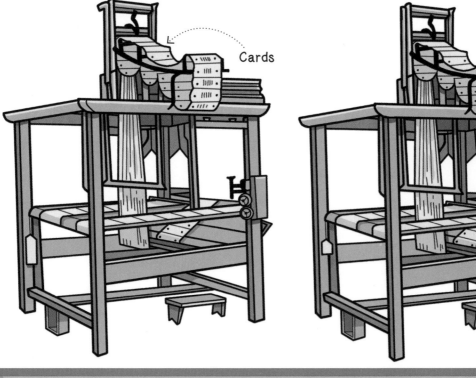

Cards

CHECK THE ANSWERS AT THE BACK OF THE BOOK!

Lovelace designed punched cards to control how the Analytical Engine worked. Try this fun punched card puzzle.

Follow the sequence on the right to get from input to output, one card at a time, by going up, down, left, or right (but not diagonally). Watch out for dead ends!

START

FINISH

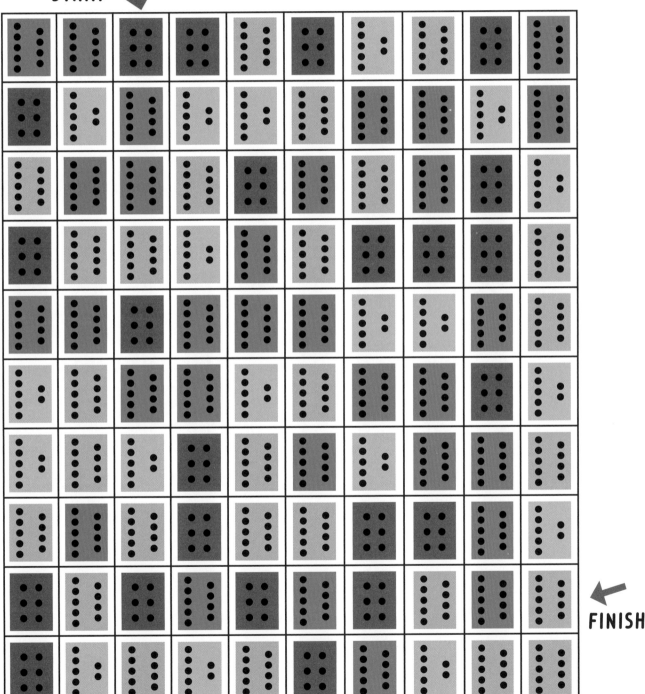

CODING PIONEERS

After Lovelace and Babbage, other coding pioneers followed. In the 1940s, at Harvard University, a new electronic computer was built, inspired by the Analytical Engine.

The new computer's full name was the Automatic Sequence Controlled Calculator. It was also known as the Harvard Mark I. It was huge—51 feet (16 meters) long and 8 feet (2.4 meters) high. It could do three additions or subtractions a second—fast in its day, but nothing compared to today's smartphones!

GRACE HOPPER

Hopper was a scientist who programmed the Harvard Mark I. She wrote a coding language, COBOL, that is still used today.

ACTIVITY

Color in the computer!

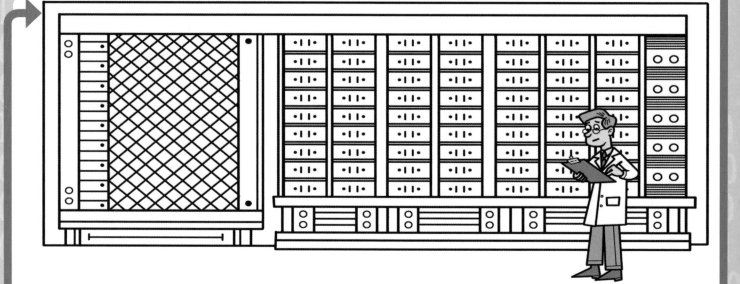

HARVARD MARK I

Programming the Harvard Mark I was a chore. Computers use a language of 0s and 1s, called binary, to process all the information that they receive. The binary commands were either slowly input via switches or fed in using paper tape with holes punched in it.

Hopper found an easier way to "talk" to computers. She designed a program to translate the input numbers into words, such as IF or STOP. This hugely reduced the time it took to program a computer!

DID YOU KNOW?

It is thought that the computer term "debugging" comes from when Hopper's team had to remove a moth from the circuits of the computer.

Can you find all of the names of these computer languages hidden in the word search grid?

SCRATCH	RUBY	PERL	ADA	PHP
PYTHON	VISUAL BASIC	COBOL	PASCAL	SWIFT
FORTRAN	C++	JAVASCRIPT	LOGO	

X	C	V	G	F	F	F	H	J	K	V	N	Y
U	T	S	C	R	A	T	C	H	O	I	M	N
H	Y	P	O	I	L	V	D	G	H	S	S	S
A	C	B	M	N	K	U	Y	H	V	U	D	K
J	H	L	O	N	B	V	C	X	Z	A	E	R
J	H	R	U	B	Y	T	G	F	T	L	H	J
U	I	K	O	L	W	Q	A	S	D	B	R	G
J	A	V	A	S	C	R	I	P	T	A	F	D
L	V	D	G	H	C	+	+	A	C	S	M	P
K	U	Y	S	V	C	D	K	J	H	I	O	Y
B	V	C	W	P	A	S	C	A	L	C	F	T
Y	T	G	I	E	Y	H	J	U	I	K	O	H
P	H	P	F	R	F	R	G	H	J	M	N	O
H	G	F	T	L	C	O	B	O	L	U	Y	N
V	C	D	K	J	H	L	O	N	B	V	C	X
Z	W	E	R	J	H	L	O	G	O	T	G	F
F	O	R	T	R	A	N	H	V	C	A	D	A

CHECK THE ANSWERS AT THE BACK OF THE BOOK!

RISE OF THE ROBOTS

Robots are machines that follow instructions from computer programs to do all kinds of jobs. They can be used to perform repetitive tasks, such as building cars, or for complex tasks like the exploration of Mars, disaster search and rescue, or surgery in hard-to-reach locations.

HENRY FORD
Ford solved the problem of making cars affordable by making them cheaper to build using "mass production."

Through mass production, cars were built by people doing the same job on each car as it moved along an assembly line.

ROBOT CAR FACTORY
Today, robots often work on car assembly lines. Here are just some of the jobs they do. Human workers program the robots. They also do many other jobs, such as checking for quality and keeping the robots running smoothly.

Cutting and shaping metal

Assembling parts

Welding and fixing metal together

Painting

ACTIVITY

The robots follow their computerized instructions exactly, repeating the same job over and over without getting tired or making mistakes. But sometimes a glitch might happen. Can you find one of these mass-produced cars that would fail a quality control test because it is not exactly the same?

TEST REPORT

Failed:

DRIVERLESS CARS

Robots are increasingly being used for jobs where they can help make our world a better and safer place. One example is driverless cars, which are robots combined with artificial intelligence!

Driverless cars are already being tested to try to reduce car accidents on our busy roads.

Sensors detect the road edges and lanes by bouncing pulses of light off of them.

Video cameras act as the robot driver's "eyes," detecting pedestrians, other cars, traffic lights, and obstacles. They also read road signs!

The Global Positioning System (GPS) uses satellite signals to locate the car. Digital maps give a safe route for the car to follow to the destination.

Radar sensors use electromagnetic waves to detect other vehicles moving nearby.

A central computer receives and processes all of the data. It makes pre-programmed decisions about how to control the car with steering, acceleration, and braking controls.

Ultrasonic sensors send out sound waves that bounce back to help detect obstacles.

Here's your chance to be the onboard computer of a driverless car. Write down the sequence of moves you need to get to the garage safely. Think like a computer and do it one logical step at a time!

It's been started for you—you can go north, south, east, or west—but don't forget to tell the computer how far to go. Find a route that avoids obstacles.

When you've finished, get a friend or family member to follow your instructions. Did they get there without a crash?

START

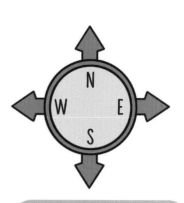

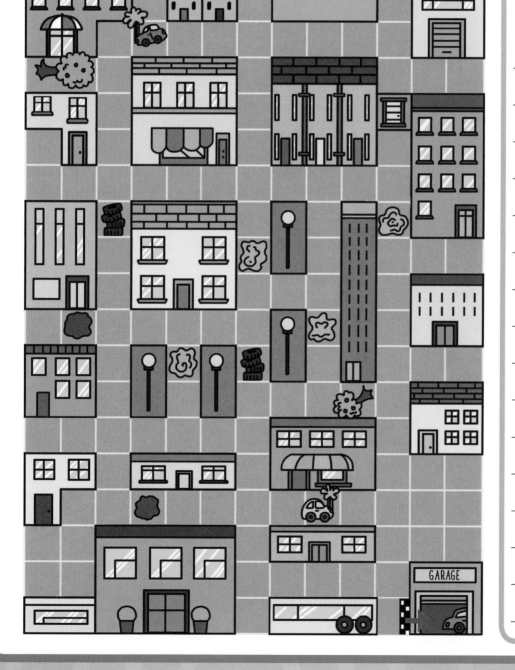

2 BLOCKS SOUTH
4 BLOCKS WEST

_____

_____

_____

_____

_____

_____

_____

_____

_____

_____

_____

_____

_____

_____

_____

GET INTO GEAR!

Engineers build machines to make things easier. A bicycle is a machine that makes traveling from point A to point B easier and quicker than walking—it uses gear power!

1 Gears are wheels with teeth that lock together so that one gear turns another. When two gears of different sizes (and different numbers of teeth) are linked together, they turn at different speeds.

This gear will turn slowly, but with lots of force.

The teeth are locked together.

This gear will turn quickly, with less force.

2 When the big gear with 60 teeth turns once, the small gear (with 15 teeth) turns 4 times (60 teeth = 4 x 15 teeth).

The small gear turns four times quicker but with 1/4 of the force of the big gear.

ACTIVITY

Look at these gears. When the small gear turns (rotates) 3 times, the large gear turns once. You'll see that 6 turns of the small gear make 2 rotations of the big gear. Do you see a pattern?

Complete the rest of the table following that pattern.

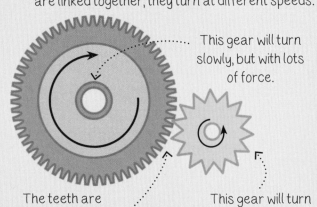

SMALL GEAR (10 TEETH)	BIG GEAR (30 TEETH)
3 ROTATIONS	1 ROTATION
6 ROTATIONS	2 ROTATIONS
9 ROTATIONS	
12 ROTATIONS	
15 ROTATIONS	

CHECK THE ANSWERS AT THE BACK OF THE BOOK!

One other property of gears is that they turn in opposite directions. This means they can be used to change the direction of a rotational (turning) force.

If you want the big hands on these clocks to turn clockwise, which way do you need to turn the drive wheel in each clock? To find the answer, add arrows to show the turning direction of each gear.

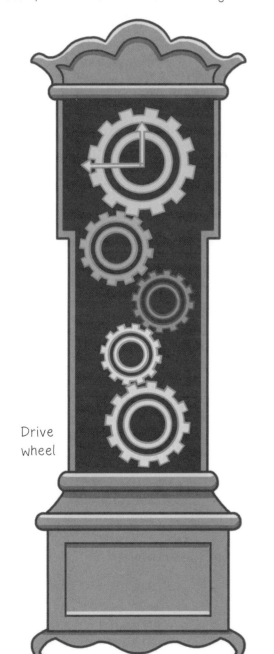

Drive wheel

Drive wheel

GEARS ON THE GO!

Bicycles use an engineering invention: a drive chain and gears! When you ride a bicycle, you turn the pedals, which turn the wheels. Gears help to spread out your effort to make that work easier—they can help you go quickly or create more power to help you go uphill.

The gears on a bicycle are joined by a chain. This means that the gear at the front turns the gear at the back in the same direction. Otherwise, you wouldn't get anywhere when you started pedaling!

In a LOW GEAR, a small front gear turns a larger rear gear. The pedals are easy to turn, but each pedal stroke doesn't turn the gear much, so you go slowly.

Smallest gear at front

Largest gear at the rear

With a HIGH GEAR, a large front gear turns a smaller rear gear. You pedal harder, but each pedal stroke turns the wheel quickly, and you go faster.

Largest gear at front

Smallest gear at the rear

ACTIVITY

When you ride a bike, you are working against the forces of gravity (those hills!), friction (bumpy dirt tracks are harder work than smooth roads), and not to mention air and wind resistance!

Look at the cartoon strip below. Which gear would you choose for each picture: 1, 2, or 3? 1 is a low gear and 3 is a high gear.

A

Gear used:

B

You're picking up speed!

Gear used:

C

Gear used:

D

Gear used:

E

Gear used:

F

You will be going fast at the bottom of the hill. Pick a gear to catch up with the speed of the whizzing rear wheel.

Gear used:

What other machines can you think of that use gears?

EVERYDAY ENGINEERING

Engineering makes our lives easier in all kinds of different ways. But it's not just machines that save us work and time; it is also the way things are designed.

Industrial engineer Lilian Gilbreth studied the way people do jobs to help make them more efficient. She once interviewed over 4,000 women to find out how kitchens could be laid out better to reduce the amount of time and energy used up doing kitchen work!

LILIAN GILBRETH

Gilbreth was the first female member of the National Academy of Engineers in the U.S. Her engineering genius was recognized with no less than 23 honorary degrees!

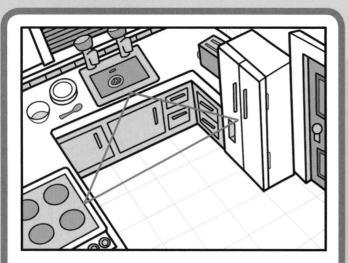

Gilbreth pioneered the idea of arranging the things used the most in the kitchen—the sink, the refrigerator, and the stove—in a triangle to minimize movements between them.

Gilbreth came up with the idea of adding shelves inside refrigerator doors and mounting light switches to walls.

She also invented something we take for granted today—a trash can that can be opened with a foot pedal, leaving your hands free!

Be inspired by Lilian Gilbreth's ideas. Look at your own home, and try to think like she did about how things could be done more efficiently. Put your ideas into practice. Can you show that your ideas work and save time and effort?

AREA OF HOME:

This could be doing the laundry, washing up, keeping your room clean, or getting your things organized for school each week.

JOB OR TASK:

RESEARCH:

How is the job done now? Is there a better way to do it? Who does the work? Ask questions. Look for other ideas. Think about where things are positioned and how they affect the job.

PROPOSED SOLUTION: YOUR NEW IDEA!

TRY IT OUT! WHAT ARE THE RESULTS?

What do you think— have you made a difference with your engineered process?

EXTREME ENGINEERING

Missions in space provide huge challenges for engineers from all fields. From launching satellites and crewed space vehicles to building and restocking the International Space Station (ISS), everything needs to be engineered perfectly.

ACTIVITY

Connect the dots to complete the building of the International Space Station!

Pressurized areas contain living space for the astronauts and the laboratories where they work.

The ISS is the largest structure built in space, occupying an area larger than a football field. It carries an international crew of six people.

Sunlight is converted into electrical energy to power the space station.

The radiators get rid of excess heat to keep the ISS at a safe temperature.

The ISS has a framework of aluminum and steel that is 358 feet (109 meters) long.

CHECK THE ANSWERS AT THE BACK OF THE BOOK!

Almost every field of engineering has been involved in creating the ISS. Can you find important ISS engineering fields in the word search below?

C	B	G	H	F	D	C	S	X	T	G	H	C
O	L	M	J	H	U	Y	T	O	I	P	L	O
M	E	L	E	C	T	R	I	C	A	L	Q	M
P	S	V	B	N	M	K	J	H	G	X	F	M
U	O	K	J	U	Y	T	I	O	P	U	I	U
T	F	G	F	D	S	A	Q	W	E	R	K	N
E	T	U	O	P	I	U	J	H	Y	T	S	I
R	W	A	X	C	V	F	D	C	V	B	T	C
K	A	H	R	O	B	O	T	I	C	S	R	A
P	R	M	K	J	Q	W	A	S	Z	X	U	T
S	E	Q	W	W	E	Y	T	G	H	B	C	I
C	H	E	M	I	C	A	L	S	A	Z	T	O
E	R	T	Y	U	I	O	P	L	K	J	U	N
H	J	K	J	H	G	B	N	M	J	H	R	S
V	B	A	E	R	O	S	P	A	C	E	A	U
O	Y	P	O	I	P	Y	T	R	E	F	L	H
M	E	C	H	A	N	I	C	A	L	X	W	V

MECHANICAL

COMMUNICATIONS

STRUCTURAL

ROBOTICS

COMPUTER

ELECTRICAL

CHEMICAL

SOFTWARE

AEROSPACE

Mechanical and Structural Engineering
One million pounds (about 4.5 million kilograms) of materials went into the construction of the ISS, about the same as it would take to build 320 cars.

Robotics Engineering
A 55-foot (16.8-meter) robot arm on the ISS can lift the weight of a space shuttle.

Computer and Software Engineering
More than 50 computers and millions of lines of code control the ISS both on board and from the ground.

Electrical Engineering
One acre (4,000 square meters) of solar panels supply electricity that runs through more than 8 miles (nearly 13 kilometers) of wire.

Chemical and Aerospace Engineering
More than 115 space flights with rocket engines powered by chemically engineered fuels have carried materials and astronauts to the ISS.

Communications Engineering
The ISS handles more than 20 times as many signals as the space shuttle did.

CHECK THE ANSWERS AT THE BACK OF THE BOOK!

ENGINEERING FUTURE

The next time you take a trip anywhere, from a ride on your bicycle to a flight in an plane, just think about how every stage of your journey has been made possible by engineers. Maybe you will be the next to join the ranks of creative and practical thinkers that will engineer the future for the world we live in!

ACTIVITY

Engineers solve problems. Sometimes they use ideas from one area to solve a problem in another. For example, one idea for a cheaper and easier way to get people and things into orbit is to ditch the rockets and build a giant elevator into space!

Why not find a problem you can solve with engineering—or discover a new use for an existing engineering idea? Who knows, maybe you will invent the car of the future or an environmentally friendly way to build a house. The future is entirely up to you!

Sketch your blueprint for a future device, a transport vehicle, or a home:

THE BIG ENGINEERING QUIZ

Now it's time to test your engineering know-how!
Check the right answers. Look back though the book
if you need to check your facts.

1

A seesaw is fun, but it's also an example of which simple machine?

a) Pulley ☐

b) Lever ☐

c) Screw ☐

2

What type of dome is made from triangular structures joined together?

a) Geographic dome ☐

b) Deodesic dome ☐

c) Geodesic dome ☐

3

What is the name of the invention that can transfer water from a low place to a higher place?

a) Artemis screw ☐

b) Archimedes screw ☐

c) Archimedes crew ☐

4

What creates extra mechanical advantage on a bike?

a) Gear ☐

b) Handlebar ☐

c) Seat ☐

CHECK THE ANSWERS AT THE BACK OF THE BOOK!

5

What kind of tires are filled with air?

a) Automatic ☐

b) Pneumatic ☐

c) Hydromatic ☐

6

Air resistance can be useful. What is the force that it exerts to slow down a parachute?

a) Drop ☐

b) Pull ☐

c) Drag ☐

7

What was the name of the world's fastest steam train?

a) The Pelican ☐

b) The Mallard ☐

c) The Duck ☐

8 What name is given to the forces that make a hot-air balloon rise?

a) Bounce ☐

b) Boing ☐

c) Buoyancy ☐

9

With an LED light bulb, what does the "LED" stand for?

a) Light-efficient dazzler ☐

b) Light-emitting diode ☐

c) Light every day ☐

CHECK THE ANSWERS AT THE BACK OF THE BOOK!

ANSWERS

Page 8
AWESOME ARCHES

Page 13
SEESAW SCIENCE

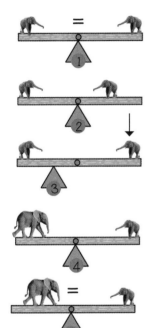

Pages 14–15
LEVERS TO LIFT

A = Class 1 lever
B = Class 2 lever
C = Class 2 lever
D = Class 1 lever
E = Class 1 lever
F = Class 1 lever

The tennis player should have the racket.

The ice hockey player should have the hockey stick.

The kayaker should have the oars.

The golfer should have the golf club.

Page 16
RAISE THE ROOF

Page 18
A SCREWY IDEA?

Page 19
WATER POWER!

Pages 20–21
TALL IS COOL

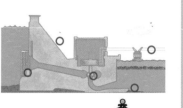
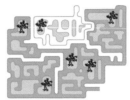
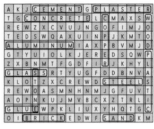

Page 23
TAKE THE ELEVATOR

Ellie lives on the second floor.

Page 25
GOING UNDERGROUND

A = Yulhyeon Tunnel, South Korea;
B = Channel Tunnel, U.K.; C = New Guanjiao Tunnel, China; D = Seikan Tunnel, Japan;
E = Lötschberg Base Tunnel, Switzerland

Page 27
WORLD OF WHEELS

Page 29
FLYING FIRSTS

1. B 2. C 3. F 4. H 5. E 6. D 7. A 8. G

Page 31
BUOYANT BALLOONS

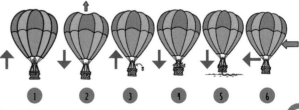

Pages 32–33
SKATEPARK SCIENCE

1. You slow down quickly, then stop.
2. Steps go up, but not so smoothly. Ouch! That hurts.
3. Get ready to catch some air!

Page 35
BRIGHT IDEAS
1. B 2. C 3. E
4. D 5. A

Page 37
EVEN BRIGHTER IDEAS!
The image on the billboard is a lighthouse.

Pages 38–39
LONG-DISTANCE INFORMATION
Wire C will get his message to Baltimore.
The message reads: What hath God wrought?

Pages 40–41
COMMUNICATIONS ON THE MOVE

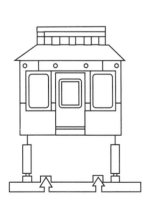

Pages 42–43
TELECOMMUNICATION FIRSTS
1. B 2. D 3. A 4. F 5. C 6. E

Pages 44–45
MATHEMATICAL MACHINES

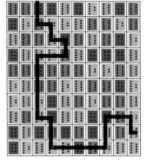

Page 47
CODING PIONEERS

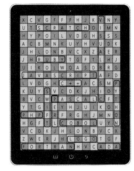

Page 49
RISE OF THE ROBOTS
The car that failed the quality control test is F.

Page 51
DRIVERLESS CARS
2 blocks south; 4 blocks west;
4 blocks south; 2 blocks east;
3 blocks south; 2 blocks west;
1 block south; 4 blocks west;
3 blocks south; 4 blocks east;
4 blocks south; 4 blocks east;
1 block south

Pages 52–53
GET INTO GEAR!
9 rotations = 3 rotations
12 rotations = 4 rotations
15 rotations = 5 rotations

You need to turn the drive wheel in both clocks counterclockwise.

Page 55
GEARS ON THE GO!
A 2; B 3; C 1; D 1;
E 2; F 3

Pages 58–59
EXTREME ENGINEERING

Pages 61–62
THE BIG ENGINEERING QUIZ
1. b 2. c 3. b 4. a 5. b 6. c 7. b 8. c 9. b